The Knights Hospitaller: The History and Legacy of the Medieval Catholic Military Order

By Charles River Editors

The order's flag

About Charles River Editors

Charles River Editors is a boutique digital publishing company, specializing in bringing history back to life with educational and engaging books on a wide range of topics. Keep up to date with our new and free offerings with this 5 second sign up on our weekly mailing list, and visit Our Kindle Author Page to see other recently published Kindle titles.

We make these books for you and always want to know our readers' opinions, so we encourage you to leave reviews and look forward to publishing new and exciting titles each week.

Introduction

The Knights Hospitaller

Brian Gotts' picture of a reenactment of a Knights Hospitaller drill

For centuries, Christians and Muslims were embroiled in one of the most infamous territorial disputes of all time, viciously and relentlessly battling one another for the Holy Land. In the heart of Jerusalem sat one of the shining jewels of the Christian faith, the Church of the Holy Sepulchre. Legend has it that this was where their Savior had been buried before his fabled resurrection. What was more, it was said to house the very cross Jesus Christ had died upon. It was for precisely these reasons that fearless pilgrims, near and far, risked their lives and made the treacherous trek to Jerusalem.

Like other secretive groups, the mystery surrounding the Catholic military orders that sprung up in the wake of the First Crusade helped their legacies endure. While some conspiracy theorists attempt to tie the groups to other alleged secret socities like the Illuminati, other groups have tried to assert connections with them to bolster their own credentials. Who they were and what they had in their possession continue to be a source of great intrigue.

The story of the Order of Knights of the Hospital of Saint John of Jerusalem, frequently shortened to the Knights Hospitaller, is long and complicated. Although the roots of the organization existed before the First Crusade, the order would not develop until 20 years after the famous call by Pope Urban II to conquer the Holy Land of Jerusalem for Christianity. Moreover, while the identity of the Knights Hospitaller was focused on the principles of crusading and military conquest, the order also focused on charitable Christian causes like the healing the sick and feeding the poor and hungry. In fact, functioning as a hospital was the original purpose of the Order before it started to militarize, yet as time wore on, such ideals would fade in the face of wealth, power, and desperation to reclaim the vestiges of prestige lost over the centuries.

The Knights Hospitaller formed in the 12th century and continue to exist in contemporary times, albeit in a considerably different form. Over the last millennium, the organization has fulfilled different roles, served varying masters, and continued to uphold the tenets of crusading even when there was no Crusade to fight. All the while, as it went through centuries of murkiness, including the development of a notorious reputation, the Knights Hospitaller continued to adapt. In contemporary times, the Knights Hospitaller could no longer be said to uphold the morals of the Crusades, but it definitely continues to adhere to the tenets of chivalry and charity. To get to this new position, however, the Order needed to undergo trials, tribulations, and years of resorting to begging.

The Knights Hospitaller: The History and Legacy of the Medieval Catholic Military Order chronicles the known history of the order and examines the secrecy and mysteries surrounding it. Along with pictures of important people, places, and events, you will learn about the Knights Hospitaller like never before.

Templar building at Saint Martin des Champs, France

The Knights Hospitaller: The History and Legacy of the Medieval Catholic Military Order

About Charles River Editors

Introduction

    The Crusades

    The Establishment of the Knights Hospitaller

    Heading West

    New Threats

    Malta

    The End of the Line

    Online Resources

    Bibliography

Free Books by Charles River Editors

Discounted Books by Charles River Editors

The Crusades

"You are called shepherds; see that you do not act as hirelings. But be true shepherds, with your crooks always in your hands. Do not go to sleep, but guard on all sides the flock committed to you...For according to the gospel, you are the salt of the earth. But if you fall short in your duty, how, it may be asked, can it be salted?" – Pope Urban II

The silky sea of sand dunes seems to stretch endlessly, the grains appearing almost golden under the glow of the scorching midday sun. A swirl of sand dances daintily across the open space as a gust of wind blows past. The scenery would have been stunning, if it were not for the swarm of black figures from afar, steadily gaining in size. The ground quakes from the pounding hooves of a thousand horses, the iron-clad men mounted on top of them brandishing their weapons and shields. Even from a distance, their thunderous cries rumble across the open space, their words as clear as the day was: "Kill all the infidels!"

Charging from the opposite side is an equally formidable sight. Hundreds upon hundreds of men in glinting armor lean forward with their reins clutched between their fists, the quilted coverings on their dressed stallions rippling behind them. Alongside them are countless men sporting turbans and conical helmets, wielding bows and arrows, spears, and mighty swords.

This is often what springs to mind when the Crusades are brought into conversation, but not only are the roots of these wars far more complex and its barbarism often glorified in modern pop culture, it spawned generations of legendary chivalric orders.

For starters, a "crusade" was a holy war, but for them to be classified as such, they had to be approved by the pope. These papal-endorsed military campaigns aimed on squashing the so-called Islamic "infidels" and enemies of Christ. But while it might appear as if the Catholics were only concerned with takeovers and forced conversions, there was far more going on under the hood than meets the eye.

Following centuries of persecution, Christianity became the official religion of the Roman Empire under Constantine the Great, and the eastern half of the Empire (which later became the Byzantine Empire) took charge of Jerusalem and the Levant, controlling the area and its flow of pilgrims. But after the collapse of Rome, the Byzantines were displaced in the early 7th century by a third "Abrahamic" (after the semi-legendary founder of Judaism, Abraham) religion known as Islam, which came out of the Arabian Peninsula. An Arab Muslim army took Jerusalem in 634 A.D., and with that the Holy Land was lost to the Christians, who mourned its loss for centuries as they remained unable to take it back.

This sense of loss was exacerbated by disputes over pilgrimage rights to Jerusalem for both Christians and Jews. Since attitudes from one Muslim ruler to the next were fluid in regard to tolerance of minority religious groups, this added to a sense of uncertainty regarding Christian and Muslim access to the holy shrines, access which was paramount to ongoing Christian and Jewish identity. While it remains unclear how tolerant Muslim attitudes in the Levant during this time were over the long-term, the lack of control of such holy sites contributed to a sense of permanent anxiety among the Christians especially. Continuing patterns of expansion and contraction on the borders of the Byzantine Empire also added to the political instability of the region.

However, in the 11th century, the Arab Muslims also lost control of the Levant to a new group coming in from West Asia through Persia and Anatolia – the Seljuq Turks. After being brought in as mercenaries in 1058, they gained control of the Abassid dynasty in Baghdad, taking most of Anatolia from the failing Byzantine Empire and also conquering most of the Levant. This was part of their original purpose of fighting the new Fatimid dynasty in Egypt.

Even at its height, the Seljuq Empire lacked a strong infrastructure and existed in a state of perpetual warfare. Syria, in the Western Levant, was loosely organized into squabbling leaders distantly swearing allegiance to Baghdad and soon began to fall apart, while Palestine was contested by the Fatimids. In the wake of the empire's growing weakness, the Byzantine Emperor, Alexius Comnenus (1056-1118), saw an opportunity to regain some territory. He had hired Frankish mercenaries before, so he sent a letter to the Pope in Rome asking for more help. What was different was the Pope's reaction, which was quite startling. He called for something new – a crusade.

It is also not entirely clear how Pope Urban II came up with the idea of a crusade to the Holy Land. Gregory had made a previous call in 1074, using the term, *"milites Christi"* (soldiers of Christ), but it had been largely ignored. It is possible that Urban had heard of the Muslim concept of jihad or holy war, and the concept of aggressive expansion through holy war was not at all unknown to Christians by that period. However he conceived the idea, Urban decided to give a speech calling his audience to go on a crusade to the Holy Land, to win back Jerusalem and cleanse the Holy Land of the Muslim threat, using the Byzantine Emperor's letter as an excuse.

It is unlikely that he was aware that he would get the response that he did, for it was unprecedented. He had perhaps hoped at best to gain some mercenaries to send to the Emperor, a few donations, even an small army. With that said, his speech was not spontaneous; he had planned it very carefully, maneuvering to bring in leaders of the crusade before announcing it.

Urban spoke to a large number of people in Clermont, France on November 27, 1095. This was known as the Council of Clermont, and the subject was the letter from Alexius. After a brief exhortation against the fratricidal violence of the knights (Urban, himself, came from nobility), Urban related the news that the Seljuqs had conquered Romania and were attacking Europe as far west as Greece. He painted a picture of Christianity in grave danger from this new, Turkish threat, even mentioning them separately from the Arabs as another group of enemies against

Christians in the Middle East.

The actual text of Urban's speech does not survive, but some chroniclers related the general tenor and structure of it, and there were no less than five accounts from possible eyewitnesses, as well as relatively fanciful and elaborate reconstructions from a generation later, such as Fulcher of Chartres' (c.1059-1127) *History of the Expedition to Jerusalem*, which was written about 30 years later. Even those completed relatively close to the time were written after the fall of Jerusalem to the crusaders. Baldric of Dol's (c.1050-1130) *Historiae Hierosolymitanae libri IV*, Guibert of Nogent's (c.1055-1124) *Dei gesta per Francos* ("God's deeds through the Franks"), Robert the Monk's (d. 1122) *Historia Hierosolymitana*, Fulcher of Chartres' chronicle, and the anonymously written *Gesta Francorum* (Deeds of the Franks) comprise the main primary sources for the crusade.

Depiction of Pope Urban II preaching the First Crusade at the Council of Clermont.

According to Fulcher of Chartres, the pope said, "I, or rather the Lord, beseech you as Christ's heralds to publish this everywhere and to pers-e all people of whatever rank, foot-soldiers and knights, poor and rich, to carry aid promptly to those Christians and to destroy that vile race from the lands of our friends. I say this to those who are present, it is meant also for those who are absent. Moreover, Christ commands it." Fulcher of Chartres has Urban II continue, "All who die by the way, whether by land or by sea, or in battle against the pagans, shall have immediate remission of sins. This I grant them through the power of God with which I am invested. O what a disgrace if such a despised and base race, which worships demons, should conquer a people which has the faith of omnipotent God and is made glorious with the name of Christ! With what reproaches will the Lord overwhelm us if you do not aid those who, with us, profess the Christian religion! Let those who have been accustomed unjustly to wage private warfare against the faithful now go against the infidels and end with victory this war which should have been begun long ago. Let those who for a long time, have been robbers, now become knights. Let those who have been fighting against their brothers and relatives now fight in a proper way against the barbarians. Let those who have been serving as mercenaries for small pay now obtain the eternal reward. Let those who have been wearing themselves out in both body and soul now work for a double honor. Behold! on this side will be the sorrowful and poor, on that, the rich; on this side, the enemies of the Lord, on that, his friends. Let those who go not put off the journey, but rent their lands and collect money for their expenses; and as soon as winter is over and spring comes, let them eagerly set out on the way with God as their guide."

Depiction of Pope Urban II

The campaign attracted thousands of hopefuls, each bearing their own agendas. The warrior class was primed and ready to fight, for that was their bread and butter, and the crusade presented them with a rare type of freedom they were not about to pass on. Their violence was not only sanctioned by the Church, they needed not be restricted by their usual employers, nor did they have to risk losing any of their territories.

The Church, recently reorganized and instilled with a new fire by the Gregorian Reform led by one of Urban's predecessors, Gregory VII, was just as ready to rise to the challenge. European Christians were taught – or brainwashed, depending on how one approaches it – to display total intolerance to heathens exhibiting "irreligious behavior." Many believed it their mission to guide these heathens to the light of God at all costs, even if it meant breaking the commandments, which in this case, they believed to be for the greater good.

Feudal Europe implemented what was known as the "primogeniture" system, wherein the firstborn sons automatically inherited the patriarch's titles and lands. This might have paved a solid path for the futures of the eldest sons in European families, but unless these firstborns were struck down by the plague or some other ill force of nature, this system left the second sons and so forth with no choice but to seek alternative venues for survival. Enterprising minds founded their own businesses and found other ways to make money, but many became hired guns, mercenaries, and the very first knights. These were the same men who were said to have made up the bulk of the crusaders.

Other reasons for enlistment were many and varied. Younger sons hoped to try their luck at conquering new lands and obtaining new properties overseas that they could call their own. Some seized the opportunity to broaden their horizons, and though this might have not been the ideal way to do it, sailing across the seas for an adventure was a motivation that sufficed for many. Kings rounded up rogue and ungovernable knights who needed an outlet for their bloodlust, and thereby rerouted their kleptomaniac itches towards enemy troops and villagers.

To medieval folks, salvation was measured by a figurative balance scale of sorts. One side weighed one's righteous acts, and the other, one's evil deeds; whichever side bore more weight indicated the salvation or damnation of one's soul. With that in mind, it was the Catholic mentality that all it took for a ticket to heaven was to even the score. This meant that racking up "righteous acts," including journeying on pilgrimages and obeying papal orders, could add the weight needed for the entry to Heaven. As a result, many sinners, particularly knights and warriors who had taken many a life, were some of the first to queue up for the enlistment. After all, Urban had assured them, "All who die by the way, whether by land or by sea, or in battle against the [Muslims], shall have immediate [forgiveness] of sins."

These knights who would fight for the cause came from all walks of life, and to cement their undying loyalty to the Christian faith, a cross was emblazoned across each and every one of their chests.

A year after Urban's famous speech, four armies of crusaders, each spearheaded by a different

European power, prepped themselves to set sail for the Byzantine territories, and scheduled the date of departure for August of 1096. In an effort to seek glory for themselves, the overeager and much less experienced army of Peter the Hermit, who christened themselves the "People's Crusade," left about a month or two before the rest of the crusaders, defying the advice of Alexios himself. When Peter's army arrived at their destination, they were greeted by the far more seasoned Muslim troops, and put out of their misery in Cibotus. Soon after came the crusaders of Count Emicho, who proceeded to wreak unchecked havoc across the Jewish communities of Rhineland. To Urban's dismay, the disobedience of Emicho, which led to the slaughter of hundreds of innocent Jews, strained Christian-Jewish relations, which was not part of the plan.

The disastrous consequences of Peter and Emicho's insubordination was precisely why each of the four crusader armies were made to pledge an oath of loyalty to the pope, to which all 3, apart from Bohemond of Taranto's forces, complied. The delay proved to be worthwhile, for in May of 1097, the crusaders stormed into Nicea, the Seljuk capital of Anatolia, and had their flags planted by the end of June. One year later, the Syrian city of Antioch was theirs.

Inspired by their string of successes, the crusaders decided it was time for the main event, and headed for Jerusalem. There, they faced off with the troops of the Shi'ite Islamic caliphate, better known as the "Egyptian Fatimids." Halfway through July of 1099, the locals caved, and to the delight of the crusaders, Jerusalem was theirs once more, closing the curtains on the First Crusade. Be that as it may, Tancred, Bohemond's nephew, had given his word to the Muslim leaders that the locals would be spared. Sadly, hundreds of innocents, including children, had fallen victim to the crusaders' swords by the end of the ordeal, which left an even fouler taste in Muslim mouths.

Medieval depiction of the Siege of Jerusalem

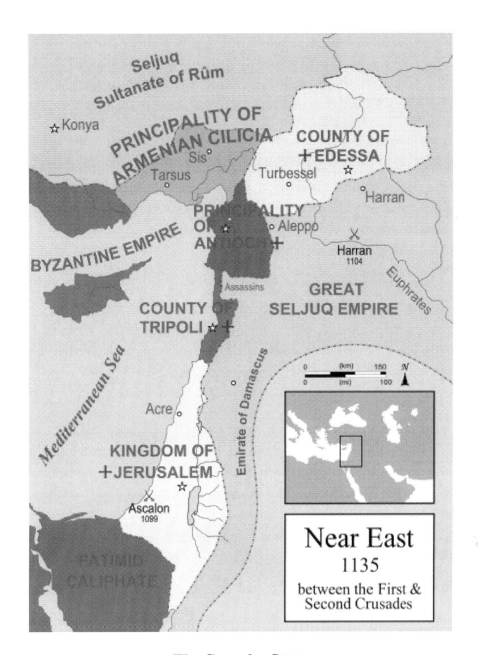

The Crusader States

    Contrary to modern Muslim views of the Crusades, contemporary Islam was not especially traumatized or disrupted by the Crusades. The First Crusade in particular had little effect on the Muslim chroniclers, and the Muslim response is found scattered through various histories of what their writers considered greater concerns.

    There were various reasons for this. First, Palestine existed in a contested area between the Abbasid Seljuq Empire of Baghdad in what is now Iraq and the Fatimid Empire in Egypt, based in Cairo. The contemporary and even later Muslim sources seemed to be confused about the origins and intent of the Crusaders. Further, both empires were not cohesive entities but squabbling groups of city rulers that existed in a fragile and constantly shifting set of alliances and rivalries. There was very little consistency of Muslim loyalty or alliance and no Pan-Arab, let alone Pan-Muslim, identity. Ibn Al-Athir, for example, believed that the Franks had been hired as mercenaries by the Fatimids against the Abbasids, not by the Byzantines to reclaim Byzantine territory. The religious motive of crusade was largely ignored.

Another important reason the First Crusade was probably downplayed by Muslim writers was the fact that the chroniclers were mostly Arabs, but most of the armies that the Crusaders fought were Turkish armies fighting for Turkish interests. The Seljuqs had recently displaced the Arab elites, so there was a disconnect between the damage the Crusaders were doing to individual rulers and the concerns of the writers recording the events. Unlike the Frankish, or even the Byzantine source of Anna Comnena, the Arab historians felt little personal involvement in the events surrounding the crusade and thus did not ascribe great importance to it.

Lastly, and perhaps most importantly, the Crusaders did not threaten the actual centers of Muslim power by passing through and claiming the contested territory of Palestine and western Syria. The distant power centers of Baghdad and Cairo were never touched or threatened, so the Crusaders were not considered a great threat by either the Abbasid Sultan or the Fatimid Caliph. This attitude would change, but not for several decades.

Meanwhile, as they were still riding the high of a victory that came much sooner than expected, many of the crusaders made the journey back home. A fraction was left behind to manage the newly conquered territories, which they called "Crusader States," or by its alternative moniker, the "Outremer," a take on the French translation of "overseas." The Crusader States consisted of dominions in Jerusalem, Antioch, Tripoli, and Edessa, where new Christian-governed castles and fortifications would rise from the ashes. Their rule was uninterrupted for about 45 years, until Zangi, the general of Mosul, and his men broke through the borders of Edessa unannounced and seized the state in 1144.

The loss of Edessa bruised the egos of the European Christian leaders back home, and 3 years later, Pope Eugene III called for a Second Crusade. These would be the first of the campaigns to be directed by monarchs – the German King Conrad III and the French King Louis VII. Hoping to score more victories, the crusaders under Conrad marched into Dorylaeum, where they had emerged triumphant during the First Crusade. Conrad and Louis then consolidated their forces at Jerusalem and set forth for the Syrian-owned Damascus with an army upwards of 50,000.

As impressive as the crusader armies were, they were no match for the Turkish forces, who had called upon Zangi's successor, Nur al-Din, for added reinforcement. By 1149, the crusaders were crushed and driven out of Damascus, abruptly concluding the Second Crusade. 5 years later, authority of Damascus was passed on to the leader of Mosul.

The wounds that came with the defeat of the crusaders were reopened in 1187. In early July that year, Saladin (the sultan of Egypt and the creator of the Ayyubid Dynasty) and his troops crossed the River Jordan and touched ground in the Kingdom of Jerusalem. Among Saladin's first orders of business was to lay siege to the fortress in Tiberias. Back in the base of the crusaders, leaders convened to brainstorm tactics that would overwhelm the growing threat of Saladin and his forces. In spite of their enormous army, the crusaders' erroneous calculations had them walking straight into the Saladin's trap.

To suppress Saladin's men in Tiberias, the crusaders had to make an excruciating trek of over 12 miles, a task made all the more difficult due to their lack of water, limited supplies, and the sweltering heat beating down on their backs. The crusaders decided to make a stopover and made it to Hattin, but just barely. There, the alarmed crusaders found that Saladin's forces had already beat them to the punch, and were standing guard over the only fresh water source, the Sea of Galilee. Saladin's men launched an ambush on the haggard crusaders, and by the end of the chaos, now immortalized as the "Battle of Hattin," almost all of the crusaders were decimated, or shackled and claimed as prisoners of war. Among the captured was Guy of Lusignan, the king of the now crumbled crusader state of Jerusalem.

For the next two months, Saladin resumed his quest to capture more territories by the Levantine coast, and soon, added Acre, Nablus, Sidon, Jaffa, Toron, Ascalon, and Beirut to his expanding empire. In September of 1187, Saladin set his sights on the grand prize, and guided his troops towards the gates of Jerusalem. Following a vicious battle that lasted 10 days incited by crusaders making a last-ditch attempt to quell the invaders, Bailan of Ibelin, who had been placed in command in the king's absence, raised his white flag. As of October 4, 1187, Jerusalem was yet again under Muslim possession.

With tensions brought forth by the ongoing tug-of-war between Muslim and Christian powers at an all-time high, it was more crucial than ever to revamp the Outremer armies, and men from even more diverse backgrounds volunteered to pitch in to help the cause. The main class consisted of the knights and their tenants-in-chief, which were barons, bishops, and abbots. In this case, the knights in question referred not just to armored men on horses, but fighting units composing of individual soldiers on horseback, and their squires, which were knights-in-training that served their superiors. Vassal knights were those who were given land in exchange for their military service, while "retained" or "household knights," as previously mentioned, were landless men who were compensated with yearly salaries. These salaries could be cashed or converted to food, clothing, horses, and other valuable supplies.

Another component to the backbone of the Outremer armies were pilgrims either reeled in by religious fast-talkers – particularly during "Pilgrim Season" between the months of April and October – or those moved by the cause. Count Philip of Flanders, who barged into Acre in 1177, was one of the top pilgrim recruiters. His army there included several earls from Meath, Essex, and other high-ranking members of the English upper class.

Mercenaries and other experts on the battlefield were hired in droves to fill in where well-meaning, but untrained farmers could not. These trained men were needed to operate crossbows and other advanced weapons, as well as to lead what would otherwise have been a band of directionless farmers in suits of armor. Many of these farmers were serfs, servants, and indentured laborers that were promised their freedom, should they join the crusade. Then, there were the Turcopoles, a name given to Christian converts of Arabic descent. Tucopoles were free men from other crusader states who bore grudges against the Turks for heavy taxes and other injustices, or those made to serve under the "Arriere Ban" by the King of Jerusalem.

Last, but not least, there were the fighting monks. These militant orders were founded with the sole mission to defend Jerusalem and its Christian pilgrims, and among the most famous of these fabled chivalric orders were recognizable names such as the Knights Templar, the Order of the Holy Sepulchre, and the Teutonic Knights. One of their most famous contemporaries was the Knights Hospitaller.

The Establishment of the Knights Hospitaller

The Knights Hospitallers Shield

At the time of the Crusades, religious knighthoods existed throughout Europe, and they were quite common around Rome and strictly Catholic kingdoms such as those of Spain and Portugal. While the Eastern Orthodox Church did spawn some of their own, these religious knighthoods were not as influential. In fact, the term "Crusades" would not be used until 1760, but even while people associate the Crusades with the Middle Ages, the practice and culture of crusading remained in Europe well after the last conflict in the late 13th century. The Knights Hospitaller themselves would continue the idea of crusading well into the 18th century after much of the medieval culture it had developed from was long gone.

Tthe Knights Hospitaller would spring up in the wake of the First Crusade, but its founders were already in Jerusalem, serving at the Hospital of Saint John to treat poor, sick Christians and pilgrims to the Holy Land currently controlled by one of the Islamic caliphates. Religious knighthoods like the Order of Knights of the Hospital of Saint John of Jerusalem garnered their beginning around 603, when Pope Gregory I commissioned a man named Abbot Probus to build a hospital in Jerusalem. The purpose of the hospital would be to treat Christian pilgrims who visited the Holy Land. The institution was successful and attended to by religious officials who cared for and treated the individuals who would arrive in the Middle East after a long pilgrimage through Europe and Africa. Around 800, the Holy Roman Emperor Charlemagne decided to enlarge the hospital and even added a library that housed rare tomes and valuable texts. Unfortunately, the hospital would only survive for another 205 years before it was destroyed along with 3,000 other buildings by Caliph Al-Hakim bi-Amr Allah.

Caliph Al-Hakim bi-Amr Allah was a member of the Fatimid dynasty, a family that ruled one of the Shia Islamic caliphates (kingdoms) exerting control throughout northern Africa. The Fatimid dynasty claimed to be the blood descendants of the prophet Muhammad's daughter Fatimah, and they originated in western Africa among the Kutama Berbers, a native ethnic group that tended to be a subservient class to Arab Muslims. Christian enemies viewed Al-Hakim bi-Amr Allah as a despotic tyrant, but many of his subjects and historians had a rosier picture of his actions. Ultimately, his destruction of much of Jerusalem would damage Christian and Muslim relations for several decades. It would only be slightly repaired when one of his successors, Caliph Ali az-Zahir, allowed Italian merchants to construct a new hospital in 1023.

This fresh institution was served by the Order of Saint Benedict and built on the site of the monastery of Saint John the Baptist. The old monastery of Saint John the Baptist had existed for 400 years, dating back to when the Byzantine Empire held power there, but it needed massive repairs. By the 11th century, it had sunk three stories beneath the ground, leaving most of its doors and windows completely obscured. Medieval texts indicate it was used as a storage house for food and water.

The Order of Saint Benedict was a monastic Catholic religious order that followed the Rule of Saint Benedict, which instructed monks and nuns to live a life of peace and hard work and presented a moderate mix of institutionalized religion and personal zeal. It was one of the most popular monastic orders, and it still exists in the 21st century. Its followers were sometimes called the "Black Monks" because of their plain black robes.

The new hospice in Jerusalem would continue its work while tensions between Christians and Muslims continued to worsen. Of particular importance during the Middle Ages were issues of territory and expansionism - the Islamic caliphates in northern Africa and the Middle East were attempting to expand northward into the Byzantine Empire's territory, and while the Byzantines had undergone a schism with the Catholic Church to the west, Christianity still tied them together. In time, Christians were also fighting with Muslims over the possession of Jerusalem, and due to rising tensions, a new monastic hospitaller order was founded during the First Crusade.

The founder of the order was Gerard Thorn, a lay brother of the Benedictine Order who served the hospice in Jerusalem.[1] He was over 70 when he was chosen and acknowledged by the papal bull *Pie Postulatio Voluntatis* in 1113 to form the new organization. In his leadership position, Gerard Thorn was required by Pope Paschal II to acquire and care for new territory and revenue throughout Jerusalem to expand the hospice and bolster the order's position in the Holy Land.

A portrait of the pope

Gerard Thorn died seven years after receiving his orders and would be succeeded by Raymond du Puy, who expanded the hospice to a functioning infirmary and slowly challenged the position of the monks in the region. Although the Benedictine Order originally just cared for sick and unwell travelers, it soon expanded its role to provide pilgrims with armed escorts and ensure they

---

[1] Jonathan Riley-Smith, *Hospitallers: The History of the Order of St John*, (Hambledon, 1999).

came to no harm in the Holy Land. Over time, this militaristic position would become a defining feature of the hospital, eventually resulting in the creation of a militia in 1118.

An 18th century engraving depicting Raymond du Puy

The militia of the Order of St. John retained a charitable character but functioned as a military organization. Raymond du Puy was the head official and divided the new militia into three ranks, including knights, men at arms, and chaplains. This militia proved exceptionally popular and was the origin of the Order of Knights of the Hospital of Saint John of Jerusalem. Its members would serve Baldwin II of Jerusalem, and they ultimately joined the First Crusade in a variety of new positions. While some served Baldwin II, others continued to aid pilgrims and attempted to keep roads clear for Christian civilians. In 1130, Pope Innocent II gifted the order its trademark coat of arms, a silver (sometimes depicted as white) cross emblazoned upon a clear field of red.

A medieval depiction of Baldwin II

It did not take long for the Order of Knights of the Hospital of Saint John of Jerusalem, occasionally shortened to the Hospitallers, to become one of the most formidable military orders in Jerusalem. Their power was rapidly recognized not only by the Catholic Church but also by individual kingdoms and wealthy nobles. Among the Hospitallers' backers was Frederick Barbarossa, the Holy Roman Emperor who would choose to make a pledge of protection to the Hospitallers in 1185. Along with this pledge came a charter of privileges that would ensure the Hospitallers received enough revenue and political status to continue their work for centuries.

For the next few centuries, the Hospitallers' rival military order was the Knights Templar, formally called the Poor Fellow-Soldiers of Christ and of the Temple of Solomon. The Knights Templar were perhaps the most powerful religious order of knights, having gained inordinate power and wealth despite the fact only 10% of its members were actual soldiers. The other 90% managed a broad economic and political infrastructure that drummed up support and revenue for the fighting in the Holy Land. That order, considered by some to be the first multinational corporation in the Western world, suffered from the seeds of distrust among members of the public who had started to hear rumors of secret initiation rituals and other unseemly escapades. King Philip IV of France, who owed the Knights Templar a lot of money, decided to use the distrust to attack the order in 1307, and the Knights Templar would be officially disbanded by the pope in 1312.

Historians debate about the full extent of the military endeavors made by the Knights Hospitaller during the twelfth century. Some believe they rivalled the Knights Templar, who are the most well-known of the monastic knighthoods, while others think they existed in the background until the thirteenth century. A lack of clear military documentation is one of the main culprits of the confusion. Many of the texts produced by the hospital of Saint John cared for by the Benedictine Order concern themselves only with the service and treatment of the sick in the region. The statutes of Roger de Moulins, produced around 1187, are a good example of this type of document. Indeed, the first actual mention of military service among the Knights Hospitaller appears over thirteen years later in 1200 in the statutes left by Fernando Afonso of Portugal.[2]

Around the turn of the 13th century, it seems the Knights Hospitaller were becoming more distinct between those who were temporary and those who were permanent members. Temporary members were often secular knights who served another lord and often came as part of a Crusade or on their own holy pilgrimage in an attempt to curry favor with God. Permanent members, meanwhile, were those who took a vow to the order and its attached hospital and monastery. These knights enjoyed many of the same spiritual privileges as that of the regular monks.

During this time, the Knights Hospitaller began promoting new distinct classes of membership in the order. There were military brothers, then the brothers infirmarians, and then the brothers chaplains. In short, the classes included those who fought, those who treated the sick, and those who dealt primarily with the spiritual health of Christians who came and went from the infirmary.[3]

Throughout the 13th century, the Knights Hospitaller and the Knights Templar developed substantial Christian fortifications throughout Jerusalem, wearing opposing uniforms that distinguished them on sight. While the Knights Hospitaller possessed red coats emblazoned with a large white cross, the Templars had white surcoats with a red cross. These standard military uniforms were approved by the papacy and lent both orders more legitimacy and credibility.

---

[2] Fernando Afonso of Portugal was the Grand Master of the Knights Hospitaller from 1202 to 1206 CE. He was the oldest son of Afonso Henriques, the first king of the newly formed Portugal. Unfortunately for him, Fernando Afonso was born out of wedlock and was banned from inheriting the crown. Instead, he joined the Knights Hospitaller after serving for a brief period with the Knights Templar. In the documents he created for the Order, he was the first Grand Master to ever mention that the Knights Hospitaller needed to engage in military service as part of their membership in the Order.

[3] Charles Moeller, "Hospitallers of St. John of Jerusalem," in Charles Herbermann, *Catholic Encyclopedia*, (New York: Robert Appleton, 1913).

A representation of a Templar

After the initial success of the First Crusade, both groups would go on to serve the Kingdom of Jerusalem, the monarchy established by Christians in the region. The kingdom's history has been notoriously difficult for historians to interpret because there were few contemporary chroniclers of the actions undertaken by the scattered crusaders. What is known is that the Church named two men, Raymond IV of Toulouse and Godfrey of Bouillon, as the leaders of the First Crusade, and when the Christians managed to take Jerusalem on July 15, 1099, the two men and the assorted other nobles met to decide how the kingdom was to be run. Although Raymond IV of Toulouse was wealthier and more important, he refused to become king, a decision chroniclers attributed to his piety and a hope that the other nobles would choose him anyway because of his humility.

Regardless of Raymond's motives, Godfrey of Bouillon was instead chosen to rule the kingdom, but he refused to take the title of king, instead preferring to be called *princeps* or his original title of *dux*. The Kingdom of Jerusalem would grow during the reigns of the next five rulers, especially under King Baldwin I, and at the peak of its power, the Knights Hospitaller possessed seven massive forts and 140 smaller properties and estates throughout Jerusalem and the nearby Principality of Antioch. Its two greatest bases were Margat and the Krak des Chevaliers, and since the order was still religious, the property was divided into priories and then further subdivided into bailiwicks and commanderies. Thus, the Knights Hospitaller appeared to play a significant role not only as the defenders of Christianity but also as a military force that could protect the palace and keep the neighboring caliphates from encroaching upon the territory of Jerusalem.

Due to their growing power, the Knights Hospitaller received recognition from powerful Christian nobles and monarchs starting in the late 12th century and continuing into the 13th century. Among the accolades received was the "Land of Severin" and its nearby mountains from Béla IV of Hungary in 1247.[4]

However, the order's enjoyment of the gift would be brief because trouble loomed on the horizon. The Kingdom of Jerusalem was unstable, and the Christians' time in power there would not last. Soon, the order would be forced to abandon its post in Jerusalem and uphold the tenets of crusading elsewhere.

Heading West

The Latin Kingdom of Jerusalem was the first crusader state and thus held a difficult position in the Middle East. Godfrey of Bouillon, a Frankish noble who ruled over territory in modern day France and Germany and the first king of Jerusalem, had set up the political system in a manner that would allow it to remain in possession of the Bouillon family. This meant the Knights Hospitaller were beholden not only to their religious order but also a specific family. The kingdom survived until 1291, when Acre was taken by the Mamluks, Arabian soldiers who managed to rise from the slave caste to become nobles. Some Mamluk enclaves would remain active as long as the Order of Knights of the Hospital of Saint John of Jerusalem itself did.

The First Kingdom of Jerusalem lasted until 1187, when the Arabian caliphate of Saladin conquered the known territory of Jerusalem and drove the Christian nobles and crusaders back. During the Third Crusade, Christian crusaders managed to take a region known as Acre in 1192, where they then established the Second Kingdom of Jerusalem. Acre was north of the central portion of the Kingdom of Jerusalem and bordered the eastern coast of the Mediterranean Sea, but it was a thin strip of land with few natural resources and little wealth, and this kingdom was destroyed in 1291. For a brief period, the Christian nobles would regain control of the city of Jerusalem and moved the capital there, but the crusaders were rapidly kicked out after two decades and once more settled in Acre. During this time, many of the crusaders and the Knights Hospitaller were of French origin due to increased religious tension and nobles seeking opportunities for political and social advancement that could not be found at home.[5]

While the fall of the Kingdom of Jerusalem had little to do with the Knights Hospitaller in the events leading up to its demise, the failure of Christian nobles to maintain control of the Holy Land would result in exile for the order, whose members would be forced to find a new home

---

[4] Martyn Rady, *Nobility, Land and Service in Medieval Hungary*, (Palgrave, 2000): p. 92.
[5] Deborah L. Arteaga, *Research on Old French: The State of the Art*, (Springer Science & Business Media, 2012): p. 206.

elsewhere. In 1187, the Knights Hospitaller were forced to leave their centuries-old hospital and move to the County of Tripoli, the last holdout of the once proud crusader state and the location of the Kingdom of Jerusalem's new capital in Acre. The Knights Hospitaller lost much of their prestige and spent much of their time attempting to defend Tripoli and Acre from unwanted invasions by Muslim caliphates and the Mongols from the north and east. When Acre was captured in 1291, the group left and sought refuge in Cyprus, a crusader state in the eastern Mediterranean Sea. Cyprus was southeast of Greece and already possessed a native population as well as some military trappings. The rocky terrain made it easy to defend but difficult to create a living.

When the Knights Hospitaller arrived in Cyprus, they immediately found themselves embroiled in the local politics of the kingdom. Jean de Villiers, Cyrpus' king, settled them in the town of Limassol, and it was there that the knights first began to equip a fleet. In short order, the knights' master, Guillaume de Villaret, decided to plot against some of the regional nobles and set his eyes upon the city of Rhodes, located on the island of the same name. The island was particularly unstable at the time, and the military leader decided to take Rhodes by force. The Knights Hospitaller implemented these designs in 1306, and Guillaume's successor, Foulques de Villaret, took the city of Rhodes on August 15, 1310 after a few years of tough campaigning and sieging. The city of Rhodes was part of the Byzantine Empire at this time and allowed the Knights Hospitaller to capture neighboring cities in the Mediterranean held by its rivals, primarily those controlled by Islamic caliphates or native peoples. The organization would also be able to dominate the port of Halicarnassus in Anatolia, and Halicarnassus became influential in subsequent years because it helped to bolster the Knights Hospitaller's navy and provided an inroad into the former Kingdom of Jerusalem now occupied by the heirs of Saladin.

On Rhodes, the Knights Hospitaller became an almost fully military order, although they still maintained and operated a hospital for the poor and the sick. The Grand Master still ruled the knights with supreme authority, but he was ultimately subject to the Grand Chapter, and he was aided in his business by various councils. He could be elected from any one of the eight "Tongues" (in French *Langues*, i.e. "languages"), or nations, into which the brothers of the Order were divided. These Tongues were the various European nations where the Order held property, and from which they gained new recruits. Each tongue had its own Bailiff, as well as one of the higher offices of the Order reserved for a brother from that nation: the Grand Commander was always from Provence, on the Mediterranean coast of modern-day France; the Marshall was always from Auvergne, also in modern day France; the Grand Hospitaller was from France proper; the Admiral from Italy; the Standard-Bearer of the Order from Aragon, in modern-day Spain; the Grand Chancellor from Castille, also in modern-day Spain; the Grand Bailiff, Germany; and the Turcoplier, the commander of the Turcopoles, England.

The Tongues were further subdivided into Priories, 24 altogether, and these into a total of 656 Commanderies. Each one was in charge of a local domain of the Order, generally a manor house with its surrounding lands. The revenues from the land, mainly the rent paid by peasants using it to farm, were divided: one portion went to support the local community of the Order, formed of a chaplain and a number of brothers; and another was sent to the Order's headquarters. The Priories were in charge of both receiving new brothers, and appointing Commanderies. The positions in the Order were held according to seniority; for example, a knightly brother attained a Commandery after three military campaigns, known as "Caravans" (Moeller, 1910).

During the 14th century, the knights solidified their hold on the island of Rhodes while still maintaining their extensive possessions in Europe, and as the other Crusader states in the former Byzantine Empire fell, over the next two centuries Rhodes would effectively become the last Crusader bastion, as well as the center for a unique military, maritime, and economic empire. Like the trading power of ancient Rhodes over a millennium earlier, the state of the knights was far more powerful than the small size of the island would have suggested. The Knights Hospitaller were also fused, in 1312, with the remnants of the Knights Templar, whose extensive properties in most of Europe they also received.

From their new island headquarters, the Knights Hospitaller additionally began to engage in privateering, becoming a naval as well as a military force. In an increasingly Muslim-controlled Eastern Mediterranean, where raids against Christian nations for pillaging and slavery were frequent, the knights used their navy not only to protect Christian ships against Muslim pirates, in particular the famous Barbary pirates, but also to mount retributive raids against the Muslims, especially the Turks. This also afforded them an added source of revenue (Bazini, 2007; Talbot 1991).

During the rule of the Knights Hospitaller, the city of Rhodos was extensively refurbished, thanks to the Order's vast wealth. Its population nearly quadrupled in size, numbering around 8,000 people, 2,000 of whom were somehow attached to the Order. About 300 were knights proper.

Much of what the Order built in Rhodes still stands today, and the medieval city of Rhodos as a whole was proclaimed a Monument of World Heritage by UNESCO in 1988. Much of the Hospitaller building program was overlaid over the former Byzantine buildings of the city. Due to the generally hostile environment surrounding its headquarters, the Order paid especially great attention to fortifications, constantly repairing, expanding, and updating the walls. In time, the knights made Rhodos one of the most important and imposing fortresses in the Eastern Mediterranean.

A depiction of Rhodos circa 1490

Bernard Gagnon's picture of the Gate d'Amboise, which leads to the medieval city

The Palace of the Grand Master

Norbert Nagel's picture of part of the Palace of the Grand Master

The Palace's courtyard

The city fortifications, according to the Byzantine plan, were in three parts, with inner and outer walls. The outer walls had a perimeter of about 2 miles and were as thick as 45 feet at places. The walls were divided into segments, each one assigned to knights from a different tongue. They were reinforced with towers, notably the famous Tower of Saint Nicholas, overlooking the military harbour of Mandraki, and bastions. They were also surrounded by a deep moat, as well as outworks and breastworks in the most vulnerable spots. The fortress was kept up-to-date with the very latest in fortification technology until the very end of the Order's rule. The *trace Italienne* ground plan, in accordance with the latest European prototypes, helped to protect the fortification against cannon fire.

W. Pietrus' picture of the location of the moat

Inside the walls, the larger, southern section of the town of Rhodos enveloped by the outer walls was where most of the population resided, including Western Europeans, Greeks, and an impressive amount of minority groups, including Armenians, Egyptians, Roma (Gypsies), and Jews. The city boasted 35-37 churches, 7 Catholic and the rest Orthodox. It was centered on the main harbor, known as the *Emporion*, which was then one of the most important ports in the Eastern Mediterranean, with two auxiliary ports in Mandraki and Akantia. The inner part of the city, the *kollakion*, was the town's administrative center, where most of the important buildings were located, such as the residence of the Catholic Archbishop, the Order's Hospital, and the Halls for the Order's various tongues. At the highest point of the city, overlaid over the old Byzantine fortress, was the Palace of the Grandmaster. This imposing rectangular edifice looms over the city to this day, and back then it served simultaneously as an administrative center, a luxurious residence, and the town's last line of defense (Bazini, 2007).

New Threats

Shortly after settling in Rhodes, the Knights Hospitaller found their crusading competition removed when Pope Clement V dissolved the Knights Templar in 1312. This dissolution had been a long time coming since many in Europe viewed the powerful Knights Templar as a threat to their own authority. The pope then developed a new papal bull which transferred much of the Templar's property to the Knights Hospitaller, which doubled its wealth, property, and political influence in Europe. At the same time, membership experienced a sharp increase as former Templars joined the Hospitallers to avoid losing their political influence and power.

As the Knights Hospitaller were developing their secular side, they continued their military endeavors by beating back Andronicus and his Turkish soldiers in 1334. This particular battle cemented the position of the order as one of the most powerful Christian organizations in the Mediterranean and caused a sharp increase in acolytes and apprentices seeking membership.

Despite the fact the order had started as a charitable hospital, the Knights Hospitaller themselves did little work treating illnesses or helping the poor by this time. These tasks were instead left to the numerous priories that dotted Europe and some sections of Africa and the Near and Middle East. Of course, this meant they lost quite a bit of their charitable reputation, and they became viewed in some places as successors of the more militant Knights Templar. The fact that the Knights Hospitaller inherited much of the Knights Templar's former holdings and properties only exacerbated the matter, even as the group gained more wealth from European nobles and commoners who wanted to be part of something greater.

Unfortunately for the Knights Hospitaller, the economic prosperity would not last. During the 14th century, feudal kings in Western Europe started to crack down on loophole exploitation when it came to property revenues. A common practice for the Knights Hospitaller was to buy land from individuals who owed dues and taxes to the crown. The order would then avoid paying the dues because they technically owed the debt, and the original individual did not pay because the property was no longer theirs. Another issue was the change in climate, resulting in colder and wetter weather in Europe, which resulted in agricultural resources dropping significantly. This led to more impoverished and displaced people relying upon charity and the Catholic Church for assistance, and as Helen J. Nicholson aptly noted, "pious donors were…less likely to give to a large, institutionalized order, and more likely to give to a local hospice where the local poor and sick were cared for…"[6] This was bad news for the Knights Hospitaller, who consisted primarily of lesser noble sons, friars, and other servants and church officials who could rely upon previously existing coffers and an organized system of support.

It seems that the Knights Hospitaller were exceptionally well-suited to governing Rhodes, given that, unlike most of its previous holders, they managed to hold onto power for over two centuries. Indeed, despite religious and ethnic differences (the Catholic, Western European knights ruled over a primarily Greek Orthodox population) and some initial tension, the knights eventually came to be well-regarded by the locals, who saw them as protectors against all foreign enemies. This was true even as the status of the Orthodox Church in Rhodes at the time was somewhat unclear. Before the final fall of Constantinople in 1453, the Byzantine emperor, along

---

[6] Helen J. Nicholson, *The Knights Hospitaller*, (Woodbridge: The Boydell Press, 2001): p. 51.

with the Patriarch of Constantinople, the head of the Orthodox Church, signed the *Laetuntur Caeli* ("May the Heavens rejoice!") agreement in 1439, uniting the Orthodox and Catholic Churches in an attempt to get help from the West against the Turks. Nonetheless, this agreement would be widely contested throughout the Byzantine Empire, and the Orthodox Church would go back on it after the fall of the Constantinople to the Turks, distancing itself once again from the West. For its part, however, the Rhodian church, although Greek Orthodox, was not within the Ottoman Empire; and in 1474, although culturally distinct from their Western overlords, it would officially declare it was still in favor of the union, thus remaining essentially Catholic. The Rhodian church would only join the "main" Greek Orthodox Church only much later, another sign that the collaboration between Orthodox and Catholic Rhodians remained strong in the face of the growth of Muslim power in Asia Minor, especially that of the Ottoman Turks (Talbot, 1991; Bazini, 2007).

Indeed, despite its initial success, the Empire of Nicaea, now effectively the restored Byzantine Empire, rapidly lost territory to new waves of Turkish invaders, in particular a new tribe known as the Ottomans. Already in the 14th century, there were many Turkish emirates along the Asia Minor coast. Despite their small fleet and low numbers, the Knights Hospitaller used their position in Rhodes as the basis to continue their Crusading activity, mainly but not exclusively against these new enemies. Demonstrating their effectiveness as pirates, the Knights of Rhodes mounted several stunningly successful raiding campaigns against the richest ports of the Orient, managing to pillage the major coastal city of Smyrna in Asia Minor in 1341, and even Alexandria, the richest port in Egypt, in 1365. The knights also conducted military campaigns against the Turkish emirates of Menthese and Aydin, and helped in the Crusaders' recovery of Smyrna for Christian forces in 1344. They also began to acquire holdings on the mainland of Asia Minor, officially taking control of Smyrna in 1374 and holding the city until it was taken by none other than Tamerlane in 1402, but not before a heroic defense by no more than 200 knights under the command of the Aragonese Iñigo de Alfaro (Moeller, 1910; Talbot 1991; Nicholson, 2001: 54).

Perhaps surprisingly, the knights' involvement with the constantly dwindling Byzantine Empire was relatively small in their early years. In 1334, they defeated an attempt by Emperor Andronicus III Palaeologus, and his Turkish auxiliaries, to retake the island. The knights also played a bit part in the interminable political strife that contributed to Byzantium's final downfall. In 1390, they sent two galleys to help Emperor Manuel II Palaeologus depose his usurper nephew, John VII. But the Byzantines were in their final days, and although the empire initially made use of the Ottoman Turks in their internal politics, with Ottomans participating in the Byzantine civil war of 1341-1347 on behalf of Emperor John VI Cantacuzene, the power balance quickly shifted. The Ottomans soon became kingmakers and began to encroach on Byzantine territory, and in March 1354, the Ottomans accomplished what none of Byzantium's Muslim foes had ever achieved. Taking advantage of an earthquake, which destroyed the fortress of Callipolis (modern Gallipoli), the Ottomans crossed over to the European half of the empire.

Although the fortress was temporarily recovered with the help of Crusaders from Savoy, the Ottomans soon expanded their territory into Europe and reduced the Byzantine Empire to a tributary, becoming directly involved in its governance (Zachariadou, 1991; Talbot, 1991; Graham, 1858: 299).

Eventually, a coalition of many of the major kingdoms of Europe, concerned about the Ottomans' rapid rise to power, organized a Crusade to stop them. Crusaders from France, Germany, and Hungary, as well as the Republics of Venice and Genoa, and even a force of Hospitallers, took to the field and faced off against the Ottomans, as well as their Orthodox Serbian vassals, at the Battle of Nicopolis on the 25th of September in 1396. The Crusader forces were routed, opening the way for Ottoman domination in the Balkans.

This would also lead to the Hospitallers' participation in the death throes of another one of the Byzantine successor kingdoms. In northern mainland Greece and modern-day Albania, the Despotate of Epirus had been one of the major kingdoms which had broken off from Byzantium after 1204. Now, in despair, the Despot of Epirus, Theodore I Palaeologus, sold the city of Corinth and then the entirety of his realms to the knights, in 1397 and 1400 respectively. As the Turks expanded into mainland Greece, the Hospitallers initially mounted a successful defense of the crucial Isthmus pass, but they were eventually constrained to abandon their new mainland acquisitions, in part by Turkish attacks, but also due to hostility from the local Greek population. These Greeks were clearly less receptive to Catholic rule than the Order's subjects in Rhodes. Despot Theodore himself eventually returned to power and seized much of his territory back from the knights and the Turks. Theodore was very close to his brother Manuel II, then Byzantine Emperor, and soon what was left of his kingdom would revert to the Byzantine Empire. This led to a rather extensive Byzantine reunification, which would prove important, even if ultimately futile in the face of the Ottoman juggernaut (Zachariadou, 1991; Tuchman, 1978: 548; Talbot, 1991 "Theodore I Palaeologos," "Hospitallers").

By now, the Byzantine successor states and the dwindling Latin kingdoms, as well as the other Muslim states in the region, were falling to the Ottomans, despite an Ottoman civil war and another European Crusade led against them that was defeated at the Battle of Varna in 1444. The Knights of Rhodes were increasingly put on the defensive, but their extensive fortifications, as well as massive revenues and of course military prowess, helped them win a number of impressive victories still. For example, in 1444 the knights repelled a punitive expedition from the Sultan of Egypt.

On the 29th of May in 1453, the final blow was dealt to the Byzantine Empire by the Ottoman Sultan Mehmed II ("the Conqueror") with the capture of Constantinople (today known as Istanbul). Mehmed subsequently proceeded to "clean up" the rest of the Latin and Byzantine successor states, conquering the last Byzantine state, the far-flung Empire of Trebizond, in 1461. This state was ruled by the old Comnenian dynasty, which had fallen back on the city after the first sack of Constantinople back in 1204 (Talbot "Trebizond, Empire of," 1991; Reinert, 1991; Babinger, 1992).

Mehmed II

The Ottoman fleet appeared on the shores of Rhodes in the Gulf of Trianda in 1480. Mehmed the Conqueror planned for his maneuvering to begin in late spring, and records indicate the attack most likely began on May 23. An army consisting of 70,000 foot soldiers, cavalry members, and assorted conscripted fighters accompanied the fleet, mercenaries were no doubt involved, and there is evidence that Mehmed the Conqueror colluded with nearby Barbary pirates to weaken the fleet of the Knights Hospitaller. The invading army was led by Mesih Pasha, one of the best tacticians in the Ottoman Empire.

A contemporary depiction of the 1480 siege

On land, the Knights Hospitaller manned their garrison and were led by Grand Master Pierre d'Aubusson. The garrison stretched along the majority of the port in the central capital of Rhodes, and there were other small pockets of defenders around the island. The main goal was to defend the Tower of St. Nicholas, which was essential for maintaining a steady defense of the two nearby harbors so the Ottoman fleet could not land.

The defenders spent their time under heavy artillery bombardment while fending off the Ottoman army on the ground, and the two-sided assault ended around June 9 when the Knights Hospitaller were victorious against the first wave of the invasion. However, the second wave came soon after, and this time the Ottomans turned their attention to the Jewish quarter of Rhodes, which rested along the eastern wall and had fewer defenses than other sections. This sector also happened to be near the bay of Akandia, which was close to an entry point into Italy and had almost no permanent defenses.

While being bombarded by the Turkish artillery, the Knights Hospitaller enlisted the assistance of the regular citizens of Rhodes and dug a moat along the internal side of the wall. They then constructed new internal fortifications to make the region more defensible, including several garrisons and towers designed to serve as strong points. The moat and new walls were key points in military tactics of the medieval era because they provided obstacles against horses and artillery. Soldiers would also need to either breach or climb the wall, which left them open to attacks by bowmen and individuals throwing stones from the top of the fortifications.

When the Ottoman offensive started in late July, the defenders and citizens all justifiably feared what would happen to them should the invaders take Rhodes. Casualties littered both sides of the garrisons and surrounding fields as the two forces clashed in almost equal numbers. Eventually, around 2,500 Turkish Janissaries managed to cross the wall, capture one of the towers, and enter Rhodes.[7] Behind them came the infantrymen. The Knights Hospitaller managed to confine the battle near the outskirts of Rhodes and enlisted the help of every able-bodied individual willing to stay and defend their home. Even the Grand Master himself was present on the frontlines, directing the knights with his lance and trying to stem the flow of Ottomans coming through the wall. Records indicate he was wounded five separate times but remained in the thick of combat.

After three hours of fighting, the Ottomans retreated and the Knights Hospitaller rested and rebuilt some of the decimated defenses. Over the next few days, the Knights Hospitaller launched a counterattack that forced the Turkish army to retreat, taking with them Mehmed's military commanders. The counterattack was so successful that the Knights Hospitaller were able to take the holy standard of Islam kept in the commander-in-chief's tent after he had fled with his army.[8]

The Ottoman army had been dealt with, but the fleet continued its attempts to enter the harbor of Rhodes and capture the city for the next week. On August 17, 1480, the Ottoman fleet finally

---

[7] Janissaries were kidnapped and enslaved individuals, primarily young Christian boys who were converted to Islam and then raised and trained in a strict order of discipline. They proved to be exceptional soldiers who served the Ottoman Emperor's household directly. Most, as slaves, were forbidden from marrying, engaging in trade, or leaving their servitude, but they could own property and were paid a reasonable wage. There is no evidence to indicate whether or not the Knights Hospitaller felt guilty about having to fight formerly Christian individuals who had been turned into warrior slaves.

[8] Elias Kollias, *The Knights of Rhodes - The Palace and the City*, p. 46-48.

retreated without garnering any success or even treasure to help mitigate the costs of the attack. By all accounts, Mehmed the Conqueror was furious and began to draw plans for a new offensive, but he would die the following year before having a chance to implement them.

The Knights Hospitaller's victory over Mehmed the Conqueror boosted their reputation once more throughout Europe, and especially in Italy and Greece, the two locations that had the most to lose from an invasion by the Ottoman Empire. The order was able to resume its activities and received several private donations as rewards and compensation for their work in protecting Christianity. Several accounts of the conflict with the Ottoman Empire have survived, primarily from eyewitnesses who may or may not have exaggerated the events. Among them is *Obsidionis Rhodiae Urbis Descriptio*, which was written by the vice-chancellor of the Knights Hospitaller, a French nobleman named Guillaume Caoursin. The work would be translated into English in 1481 and disseminated throughout European courts and monasteries.

Malta

Without the Ottomans posing much of a threat, the Knights Hospitaller did little military campaigning for the next 30 years. Instead, they continued to have skirmishes with the Barbary pirates and built a political and commercial base for themselves in Rhodes. Records show that in 1494, they constructed a new stronghold, this time on Halicarnassus. This new fortress was the Petronium, and it was even strengthened and buttressed with pieces of the ruined Mausoleum of Halicarnassus that, while still standing, was in terrible shape.[9]

---

[9] The Mausoleum of Halicarnassus is considered one of the Seven Wonders of the World, meaning the fort was built with pieces of an architectural legend.

The Petronium

By the time of Suleiman the Great's ascension, the Ottoman Empire was already in good condition. It was politically stable, culturally flourishing, dominating trade in the area, and in possession of a superior military organisation, which allowed Suleiman I to continue his predecessors' work without much need to change the direction of the empire. Selim's aggressive rule left the Janissaries efficient and strong, the Mamluks defeated, and the holy cities subsumed into the empire. The Republic of Venice in the west, as well as the Safavids in the east, had been weakened, and for the first time, the Ottoman had a fleet able to challenge old trade structures and rise as a new dominant power on the seas. Things were going well, and Suleiman intended to keep it that way.

Suleiman the Magnificent

Suleiman had expansionist dreams—not unlike any other Ottoman sultan—and he was immediately thrown into action when an uprising started in Damascus in 1521. Suleiman personally went to fight his first battle as sultan and won quite easily when the treacherous, Ottoman-appointed governor was killed in the same battle. Later that year, Suleiman rode west aiming for Belgrade, one of the last Christian strongholds in Ottoman territory, under the rule of the Hungarian Kingdom at the time. By using both infantry, cavalry, and heavy siege armaments from land as well as a flotilla of ships hindering potential aid arriving via the Danube, Belgrade's futile attempts to defend itself were of little use, and the city fell in less than two months.

The Ottoman expansion continued targeting Christians, as had been the habit for many hundreds of years. Though the founders of the Ottoman Empire—Osman and his first successor, Orhan—had not been strong advocates of the Islamic faith, religion was an integral part of both private and official life in the empire. In the 16th century, it had become such a strong, defining element that most campaigns led by Ottoman sultans were religious in nature, whether against the old Christian enemies or the new Shiite Muslim opponents in the east. Because of this, Suleiman was compelled to march south toward Rhodes to expel the Knight Hospitallers who had resided on the island since the time of the Crusades. The knights had become a nuisance to many groups of surrounding Muslims of late, mostly through acts of piracy. The knights captured ships from the Ottomans and other Muslim states, stealing valuable goods and cargo and enslaving the Muslim crews. They also attacked Muslim ships passing by on their way to perform Hajj, the Muslim pilgrimage, in Mecca. This was something Selim had failed to put to an end during his reign and which Suleiman made his priority.

The residing knights had already anticipated an attack from the Ottomans and had been fortifying their capital using Muslim slaves as laborers. By the time of the siege of Rhodes, the capital of the island had three rings of stone walls as protection and the knights were prepared for the vengeful Ottomans heading their way. Starting with a fleet of 400 ships followed by an army of 100,000 men led by Suleiman himself, the siege started in June 1522. The fortifications resisted the fury of Ottoman bombings and gunpowder mines, and the inhabitants of Rhodes refused to acquiesce to Suleiman. After months of waves of invigorating progress followed by demoralising setbacks, both sides were exhausted. No other Christian allies had come to aid the Knights Hospitallers when the Ottomans had a slight upper-hand in the internecine siege. Through major losses, it was just a matter of time before the walls would eventually give in.

A medieval depiction of Turkish Janissaries laying siege to Rhodes

A truce was negotiated in November, but the population's demands for safety and privileges were too high for Suleiman to accept. The siege continued for another month until the civilians had finally had enough and pressured the knights' Grand Master to negotiate peace. Suleiman showed no acrimony and gave the knights—as well as the civil population—generous terms. The knights were given 12 days to leave and allowed to take weapons, personal belongings, and any religious relics they wanted along with them. The population was given the possibility to live under Ottoman rule for three years and were able to leave whenever they wanted during this trial period. The people who chose to permanently settle on the island would be free of taxes for five years and guaranteed freedom of religion under the promise that no churches would be desecrated and turned into mosques. Most of the population stayed on the island, now a part of the Ottoman Empire. The knights marched from the city in January of the following year onto Suleiman's ships heading for Crete. He had chosen not to annihilate the Knights Hospitaller, something many of his predecessors might have done, after the successful siege. His aim had been to control trade in the Mediterranean, a goal he achieved in the name of Islam. Instead of instigating fear and hatred, his prudent nature and diplomatic solutions earned him respect across Europe and Central Asia, which was uncommon for a conqueror of his measures.

Although they ultimately lost, the knights had awed both Muslims and Christians through their bravery. According to the terms of surrender, the Sultan allowed them to leave the island, along with a large number of civilians who chose to opt out of Ottoman rule. Pope Hadrian VI even proclaimed the Grand Master a Defender of the Faith.

After being forced out of Rhodes, the Knights Hospitaller spent seven years residing in Sicily without an official home or garrison, but around 1530, Holy Roman Emperor Charles V decided to gift the order the islands of Malta and Gozo, as well as the port city of Tripoli in North Africa, as a fiefdom. The emperor's motivations varied, but most historians believe he granted the knights the territory partially out of religious devotion and mainly to protect those regions from the looming Ottoman threat. Both Malta and Gozo were between Sicily and the North African coast and were prime locations for the Ottoman Empire to try to make their next move to gain inroads into Europe.

The movement to Malta was inexpensive for the Knights Hospitaller, who were asked only to pay an annual fee of a Maltese falcon, which became known as the Tribute of the Maltese Falcon. This falcon was to be sent to the Viceroy of Sicily on All Souls' Day each year. The text of the fiefdom grant read, "[W]e grant, and of our liberality we bountifully bestow upon the aforesaid Very Reverend Grand Master of the Religion and Order of Saint John of Jerusalem, in feudal perpetuity, noble, free and unencumbered, our cities, castles, places and islands of Tripoli, Malta and Gozo, with all their cities, castles, places and island territories; with pure and mixed jurisdiction, right, and property of useful government; with power of life and death over males and females residing within their limits, and with the laws, constitutions, and rights now existing amongst the inhabitants; together with all other laws and rights, exemptions, privileges, revenues and other immunities whatsoever; so that they may hereafter hold them in feudal tenure from us, as Kings of both Sicilies, and from our successors in the same kingdom, reigning at the time, under the sole payment of a falcon; which every year, on the Feast of All Saints, shall be presented by the person or persons duly authorized for that purpose, into the hands of the Viceroy or President, who may at that time be administering the government, in sign and recognition of feudal tenure; and having made that payment, they shall remain exempt and free from all other service claimable by law, and by custom performed by feudal vassals."[10]

From their new vantage point, the Knights Hospitaller were able to continue their work of religious devotion, resist the Muslims to the east and south, and interfere in the politics of Europe depending on the nationality of their current Grand Master and which nations supported the order. There is some evidence to indicate that the knights assisted Iacob Heraclid, a native of Malta, in managing to create a military foothold in Moldavia. The order also bolstered its navy and continued to skirmish with Barbary pirates and the Ottomans as they attempted to expand into the western Mediterranean Sea. In 1565, the Knights Hospitaller were attacked by Suleiman, who sent 40,000 soldiers to attempt to wrest control of Malta from them. This would become known as the Great Siege of Malta, lasting from May 18-September 11.

The first two months of the siege were devastating for the Hospitallers, who lost most of their cities and half of their 8,000 knights. Resources were scarce and supplies were running low, resulting in starvation and disease. By August 18, the lines were ready to crumble, especially since the series of fortifications were spread out and difficult to defend. No help was forthcoming from the Viceroy of Sicily, who was under no obligation to assist because of the vague wording of the orders he received from King Philip II of Spain. Indeed, it could have been disastrous for Sicily since sacrificing their own troops would have left Sicily and Naples open to Ottoman invasion. When told to withdraw to spare the rest of the order, Grand Master Jean Parisot de Valette refused and held his ground, and finally, after months of ignoring the issue, the Viceroy of Sicily sent aid to the Knights Hospitaller after being badgered by his outraged officers.

On August 23, the Ottomans launched their last assault upon Malta. The fighting was intense, and even wounded knights participated. The Ottoman army was unable to break through the Order's fortifications, as the garrison had repaired the worst of the damages and any breakages to avoid giving the Ottomans an advantage. Furthermore, the invaders themselves were suffering from a variety of diseases that spread through their cramped and crowded quarters. Food was running short and ammunition was limited – it would not be until the 16th century that guns were common on the battlefield.

Without a clear path to victory, Ottoman morale was low, especially since many of the skilled commanders who had accompanied the invaders were already wounded or killed in battle. The remaining officers were incompetent, failing to properly utilize their fleet, intercept communications between Malta and Sicily, and inform the rest of the Ottoman Empire about the situation.

On September 1, the Ottoman troops tried once more to breach Maltese fortifications, but the attempt was feeble. The remaining commanders met together and discussed the failures to take

---

[10] The Sovereign Military Hospitaller Order of St. John of Jerusalem of Rhodes and of Malta, *Special Review Commemorating the State Visit to Malta by His Most Eminent Highness The Prince and Grand Master Fra' Angelo de Mojana*, 1968.

the island, as well as news that Sicilian reinforcements were set to arrive from Mellieha Bay. Since the officers had failed to intercept messages between Sicily and Malta, they did not know that the reinforcements consisted of only a small force and were unlikely to be a major threat. Thus, the Ottomans cancelled their siege and abandoned Malta on September 8.

After the Great Siege of Malta, the Knights Hospitaller would have no more decisive victories against their enemies, which should come as no surprise given that by the time the Ottomans left, the order only had 600 men capable of fighting. Some historians attribute the knights' victory to sheer luck, while others cite the effort and willpower it took to man the defenses. Perhaps the best way to put it is that the knights earned the victory, but they expended themselves almost entirely in doing so.

The Knights Hospitaller set about restoring and rebuilding Malta, and since the capital city had been razed, they developed a new one and named it after their Grand Master Valletta, who had withstood the siege alongside them and led them to victory. Around 1607, the office of the Grand Master was honored once more, this time by being granted that status of a Prince of the Holy Roman Empire (*Reichsfürst*). In 1630, the office was honored once more, this time granting the position ecclesiastic equality with cardinals.

In addition to building Valletta, the Order commissioned several works of art, and stories from the siege inspired painters in other Christian kingdoms. Some of the greatest works inspired by the siege can be found in the Hall of St. Michael and St. George in the new Grandmaster's Palace built in Valletta. Other depictions would appear in London.

While the Order of Knights of the Hospital of Saint John of Jerusalem had found a new, semi-permanent home on Malta, they had lost their original reason for existing: crusading in the Holy Land. At this point, it was no longer possible given the lack of military and financial power, the strength of the Ottoman Empire, and the fact so many of the Crusades were abject failures.

Without a means to acquire the Holy Land and with almost no financial support from European nobles, the Knights Hospitaller focused on policing the Mediterranean Sea and stopping the advance of the Ottoman fleet and the Barbary pirates who raided European ships. As a result, the actions of the Knights Hospitaller in the Mediterranean have been referred to by some historians as the *Reconquista* of the Sea.[11]

The knights primarily set out to protect Christian merchant shipping sailing to and from the Levant with goods destined for Europe. At the same time, they targeted the ships of the Barbary pirates, whose most frequent cargo were Christian slaves taken from places like the Iberian

---

[11] The Reconquista was a period in Iberian history when the Christian kingdoms that had been displaced decided to fight back against the ruling Islamic caliphate, resulting in seven hundred years of warfare and the eventual combination of the kingdoms into Portugal and Spain. The period derives its name from the premise of the Reconquista which was the taking back of what was rightfully Christian from Muslim invaders.

Peninsula and North Africa. However, there was not much money to be had in these types of missions, and by assuming the role of protector of the Mediterranean, the Knights Hospitaller took a job traditionally handled by Italian city-states like Genoa, Pisa, and Venice without receiving additional income. Over time, the knights became disillusioned and adhered less to their Christian principles, subsequently earning their money by raiding Muslim ships of all types.[12] Such profits allowed the knights to live more luxuriously, and many started to marry local women and join the navies of other European countries for experience and more income.

The order was not alone in experiencing a decline in religious attitudes and righteousness. In the 16th century, Catholicism rocked by Martin Luther and John Calvin, and the Reformation and Counter-Reformation led to religious warfare between Christians, destabilizing the Catholic Church. More and more people were moving away from traditional Christianity in favor of a system that relied less on a special class of religious individuals and the rule of people like the pope, and a religious army was no longer important to many nations. With that, the number of volunteers and tributes from European countries declined sharply, and the knights were compelled to become more tolerant of other Christian sects. In fact, the knights looked to Jews as potential members, and they sought out England as one of their member states.

The Knights Hospitaller would have a complicated relationship with the rulers of England. The order and their associated monasteries had been actively suppressed and prosecuted under King Henry VIII, who had abandoned the Catholic Church in favor of creating the Church of England so he could divorce his first wife, Catherine of Aragon. However, the Knights Hospitaller needed more members and funding, so they petitioned his daughter, Queen Elizabeth I, for the re-admittance of England. At the same time, the order created a new *langue* in the region of Germany, which included Protestant and Evangelical members in addition to traditional Roman Catholics.

Ultimately, these moves were not enough to save the Knights Hospitaller from a perceived and very real moral decline. The order was called numerous names throughout history, but around the start of the 16th century, they were widely known as "mercenary sea dogs."[13] A major problem experienced around this time was that the knights were losing their independence and holy calling, and they were more than willing to fight as mercenaries for European countries willing to pay them. When the order was originally created, the goal was to be independent of the European powers to avoid becoming beholden to one and facing the possibility of being sent to war against fellow Roman Catholics, but in the 16th century, as more knights went to work for France and became involved in the Franco-Spanish naval skirmishes of the time, they were doing just that. Another issue was that France was, for many decades, on friendly terms with the Ottomans.

---

[12] Peter Earle, *Corsairs of Malta and Barbary* (London: Sidgwick & Jackson, 1970): p. 97–109.
[13] Paul Walden Bamford, "The Knights of Malta and the King of France, 1665-1700," *French Historical Studies*. 3 (4) (1964): 429–453.

To many historians and even the order's contemporaries, its members' decision to join the French navy demonstrated how many of them had eschewed their holy mission in favor of financial profits. Many of the knights, however, adopted a different view - while quite a few admitted that joining the French navy was an excellent opportunity to earn extra money, enjoy debauched ports, and break up the monotony with short trips throughout the Mediterranean, others thought it gave them a new avenue to serve the Catholic Church, and while the French often took action against Spain, the order did not seem perturbed by the sudden shift to fighting other Christians. Instead, since many of the knights were French, it seemed an act of loyalty and even patriotism.

Justifications aside, modern historians are not so kind in their appraisal of the knights when it comes to this shift in their priorities. Among them are Paul Lacroix, who noted, "Inflated with wealth, laden with privileges which gave them almost sovereign powers... the order at last became so demoralized by luxury and idleness that it forgot the aim for which it was founded, and gave itself up for the love of gain and thirst for pleasure. Its covetousness and pride soon became boundless. The Knights pretended that they were above the reach of crowned heads: they seized and pillaged without concern of the property of both infidels and Christians."[14]

While the Knights Hospitaller attempted to make money aiding the French navy and fighting Barbary pirates, they actually made the situation worse. European nations refused to grant money to the organization because they believed the knights were acquiring plenty of funds through their exploits, so the order was thrown into a vicious cycle of needing money, failing to earn grants from Christian nations, and being forced to raid across the Mediterranean, all of which ensured their former allies were unwilling to grant any financial assistance. By the 17th century, the order found itself in a state of almost perpetual poverty since it needed money to pay for its fortifications on Malta and continue to serve Sicily. The situation would only worsen in 1618 with the start of the Thirty Years' War as the European nations became preoccupied with fighting one another.

By the 1640s, things were bad enough that officials in the order wrote to King Louis XIV of France, who was their only significant benefactor. The letter, composed and sent from Valletta to Paris, was simple and clear: "Italy provides us with nothing much; Bohemia and Germany hardly anything, and England and the Netherlands for a long time now nothing at all. We only have something to keep us going, Sire, in your own Kingdom and in Spain."[15] In essence, the order was reduced to begging for money.

Despite the plea, most historians suspect the situation was not as dire as the council in Valletta made it sound, given that corsairing was still a profitable business. Nonetheless, it is clear from

---

[14] Paul Lacroix, *Military and Religious Life in the Middle Ages and the Renaissance*, (New York: Frederick Ungar, 1964), p. 188.

[15] D.F. Allen, "Charles II, Louis XIV and the Order of Malta," *European History Quarterly*, 20 (3) (2016): 323–340.

some surviving documents that the knights were not content with their new lot in life and wished to once again return to a more respectable and holy mission. Of course, these sentiments were not strong enough to deter them from profiting by policing and conducting raids against ships deemed "infidels." The common practice was to attack the ship, kill or capture the crew, and then take the cargo for personal use or to sell in Europe. Most of the individual knights were able to keep the profits despite having taken vows of poverty upon joining the order.

Like everything else for the Knights Hospitaller, such economic prosperity would not last. In 1789, the French National Assembly abolished feudalism and with it any support for the order, which relied upon dues and tithes. The text of the decree read, "V. Tithes of every description, as well as the dues which have been substituted for them, under whatever denomination they are known or collected (even when compounded for), possessed by secular or regular congregations, by holders of benefices, members of corporations (including the Order of Malta and other religious and military orders), as well as those devoted to the maintenance of churches, those impropriated to lay persons and those substituted for the portion congrue, are abolished..."[16] The French Revolutionary Government would also take all of the assets belonging to the order in France in 1792.

It was not solely on the waters of the Mediterranean that the Knights Hospitaller earned their newfound notoriety. From the moment they set foot on the shores of Malta, the knights were disliked by the native population, which viewed these new unchosen masters as little more than exploiters and bullies. The Knights Hospitaller would stay for 268 years, during which they would exclude the natives from important political positions and decisions, control the economy, and even take advantage of the native women.[17] The Maltese nobility did little to dissuade the Knights Hospitaller from staying since the presence of new individuals boosted the local economy and pushed Malta to a new position of political importance for a short time.

On Malta, the Knights Hospitaller continued many of the acts that originated with the order, including the building of new hospitals to treat sick and injured Christians who inhabited the island. These hospitals had the added side effect of causing the native Maltese and Italian to be supplanted by French, which was spoken by the monks and knights tending to the patients. While the native Maltese continued to speak their language amongst themselves, French was the new language of commerce and political prestige, mirroring a situation that had occurred in England centuries prior. At the same time, the former crusaders also worked to construct watchtowers and fortresses for added military protection.

In time, the knights permanently changed the landscape of Malta, especially with the creation of the new capital of Valletta. That city would become a center of art and learning built through

---

[16] J.H., Robinson ed., "The Decree Abolishing the Feudal System," *Readings in European History 2 vols*, Boston: Ginn, 2 (1906): 404–409.
[17] John Sugden, *Nelson: The Sword of Albion* (illustrated ed.), Random House, 2014 p. 122.

the labor and funds supplied by the Knights Hospitaller in conjunction with the indigenous locals. Some of the best hospitals could be found there, including the Sacra Infermeria, which could hold 500 patients. In 1761, a massive public library appeared, and the knights built a new university in 1779. In 1786, the university was expanded with a new School of Mathematics and Nautical Sciences.

However, resentment towards the order continued unabated on Malta, even among the nobility. This was due in large part to the fact that the knights, despite becoming more open to different sects of Christianity, continued to hold prejudices based on race and ethnicity. The native Maltese, including nobles, were banned from admittance to the order, and that situation would not change for many years.

In 1798, none other than Napoleon Bonaparte arrived, and he demanded that the Grand Master allow his entire fleet to enter the port to resupply. Grand Master Ferdinand von Hompesch zu Bolheim rejected the request, stating that the knights had a strict limit on how many foreign ships could enter the port at a given time. Instead, he told Napoleon that the ships could enter by twos in order to pick up food and water. Napoleon, who was taking a considerable army to Egypt, knew that it would take forever for his fleet to be provisioned that way, so instead of complying, he ordered his ships to fire their cannons against Malta. On June 11, the soldiers disembarked and attacked seven different points on the island, and after a few hours, the Knights Hospitaller and the Maltese surrendered.[18]

---

[18] Juan Cole, *Napoleon's Egypt: Invading the Middle East*, Palgrave Macmillan., 2007, p. 8–10.

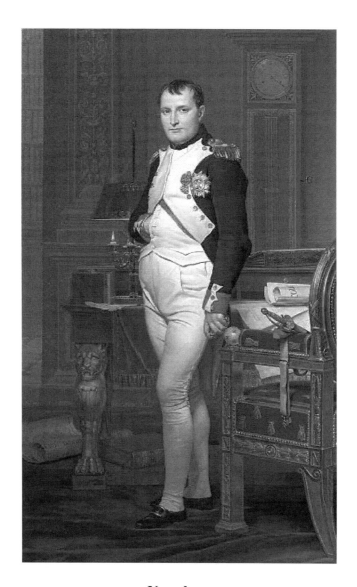

Napoleon

Ferdinand von Hompesch

A depiction of Napoleon landing on Malta

Napoleon and the Grand Master met in Valletta to discuss the terms of surrender. Given that the Knights Hospitaller were vastly outnumbered and had lost western Malta in the skirmish, they had no choice but to accept Napoleon's terms, which involved the order leaving Malta. Hompesch left for Trieste and resigned as Grand Master of the Knights Hospitaller, while the remaining knights dispersed and were unable to exist in any organized fashion for many years. Later, Napoleon would remark, "The place certainly possessed immense physical means of resistance, but no moral strength whatever. The Knights did nothing shameful – nobody is obliged to perform impossibilities."

Napoleon declared Malta a French dependency and busied himself with establishing a republican administration while he looted the island's treasury on behalf of the Republic. The possession of Malta almost ensured possession of the Levant, and it was at that point that Napoleon saw fit to reveal to his army what most were in any case beginning to suspect: their final destination was Egypt.

The End of the Line

In the wake of being kicked out of Malta, the Order repeatedly pled with various European governments for stability and the opportunity to reestablish itself, but these requests were often rejected. Some knights were offered asylum by the Russian Emperor Paul I, and this group, sheltered in Saint Petersburg, would develop into a unique Russian tradition of the Knights Hospitaller and come to be recognized as members of the Russian Imperial Orders.

The rest of the knights were not as lucky. By the early 19th century, the order was scattered throughout Europe without a base of power or centralized location. Although Sweden had offered the Knights Hospitaller the island of Gotland, the deal was rejected because they felt it meant giving up their claim to Malta. At the same time, the majority of the priories had been lost due to splits between Catholicism, Protestantism, and Evangelism along with a general decline in interest in the religious life. By 1810, the order was 90% funded by the Russian Grand Priory established under Emperor Paul I, and only 10% of the Knights Hospitaller's income came from more traditional sources in Western Europe.

   This situation would continue until 1879, when Pope Leo XIII declared a new Grand Master for the order and bolstered its position as a humanitarian and religious organization. Before 1879, the Order of Knights of the Hospital of Saint John of Jerusalem had undergone a significant change of name following part of the order's decision to settle in England around 1834. To get to that point, the order went through a series of failed attempts to become involved in military activities, including fighting in the Greek Civil War. In 1823, the Knights Hospitaller attempted to raise money to build a new territorial base for the order so they could assist in the Greek War of Independence, and to get the funds, members of the order issued bonds throughout London to demobilized British soldiers. The goal was to develop a mercenary army that used cheap war surplus supplies that were not in use. At the same time, the Knights Hospitaller worked with Greek rebels to quietly transfer Greek islands to the possession of the order, including Rhodes, to form a base.

Pope Leo XIII

Unfortunately – or perhaps fortunately, depending on one's point of view – the actions of the Knights Hospitaller were discovered by the press, and word got out that they were attempting to secure private funding for a mercenary army designed to interfere in another nation's conflict. The French monarchy withdrew its support of the Council of the French *Langues* – the French chapter of the Knights Hospitaller – and bankers refused to offer any funding to the organization.[19] Following this failure, the council controlling the order was reorganized to accommodate a different political structure, although the focus of the leadership remained on finding a new base for the Knights Hospitaller. The Marquis de Sainte-Croix du Molay ascended to the leadership and commanded the order to try to raise money to develop a Mediterranean homeland for the knights. This new attempt tried to secure donations from individuals throughout England and its dominated territories with promises of membership in the order, but it was ultimately unsuccessful. The order set up shop in England and worked through several of its old priories and meeting houses to try to drum up support. Over a span of 40 years, the Order of Knights of the Hospital of Saint John of Jerusalem based in England would undergo several name changes, resulting in the final title of the Grand Priory in the British Realm of the Most Venerable Order of the Hospital of Saint John of Jerusalem in 1936.

Meanwhile, the remaining section of the order chose to settle in Rome around 1834. While there, they abandoned their military pursuits in favor of their original work of building hospitals and tending to the sick and poor of the city. The new hospital assisted in numerous welfare activities, including supplying medicine and treatment to soldiers during World War I and World War II. The man responsible for the significant expansion of the hospital's services was Grand Master Fra' Ludovico Chigi Albani della Rovere, who would serve in the position from 1931-1951.

---

[19] H. J. A. Sire, *The Knights of Malta*. Yale University Press, 1996, p. 249.

Chigi

The divisions between the Russian, English, and Italian segments of the Order were not the only separations experienced by the knights over their long history. During the Reformation in the 16th century, many of the German commanderies chose to declare allegiance with the Knights Hospitaller while also choosing to convert to evangelical Christianity. This resulted in a unique German branch of the Knights Hospitaller called the Order of Saint John of the Bailiwick of Brandenburg. The Protestant branch of the order then spread throughout many of the countries that embraced Protestantism, and eventually expanded to cover all six of the inhabited continents around the world. To this day, this section of the order features members in diverse locations like Poland, the United States, Mexico, Colombia, Namibia, China, and Australia.

At the same time, some branches of the Order of Saint John of the Bailiwick of Brandenburg separated from the original group, most notably in the Netherlands and Sweden. These separate orders became independent during World War II and have their respective national kings as the symbolic and honorary commanders of the Knights Hospitaller.

Despite these separations, many of the segments of the Knights Hospitaller continue to work together in the present day. For example, the Protestant orders in Sweden, the Netherlands, and Germany came together in 1961 to form the Alliance of the Orders of Saint John of Jerusalem. While still independent, the organization works heavily with the Roman Catholic Sovereign Military of Malta (full name the Sovereign Military Hospitaller Order of Saint John of Jerusalem, of Rhodes and of Malta). This section, often shortened to the abbreviation SMOM, is considered the oldest surviving branch of the original Knights Hospitaller, as well as the longest-lasting and oldest order still based on the principles of medieval chivalry.[20] The sovereign status of the order is recognized by many international bodies like the United Nations.

Today, the varying branches of the Knights Hospitaller continue to maintain diplomatic relationships with 107 separate countries as well as more official relations with the European Union and six additional nations with little to no membership. They retain membership in and send delegations to the meetings of the European Union and other organizations while also being capable of issuing passports, currency, vehicle registrations, and even stamps. At the same time, the knights continue to develop, staff, and create new hospitals, medical centers, first aid corps, and even daycare centers for people of all backgrounds. As of 2019, the total membership of the Knights Hospitaller was 13,500 individuals, with an additional 42,000 trained medical staff and 80,000 volunteers. While the order strives to help everyone, its specialty focuses on caring for the victims of natural disasters and armed conflicts, as well as refugees. The distribution of basic supplies and medical equipment is also tantamount to the order's new mission.

As their history makes clear, the Knights Hospitaller's story is a long and complicated one, full of crucial victories and disastrous defeats. The original hospital in Jerusalem tended to by monks has developed into an international organization that almost met its end hundreds of years ago, and even though the order continues to exist, its primary mission has undergone numerous changes that reflect the positions of crusading, the Catholic Church, and European relations. Historians of the Knights Hospitaller could argue that the changes experienced by the order are reflective of modifications to the beliefs of Christianity in general. While the order started as a highly disciplined monastery assisted by dedicated knights, it became lax with its restrictions following the Reformation and the schism that would divide Europe between Catholics and Protestants. The decision of the order to stop being strict also reflected changing attitudes towards religion throughout Europe as people focused less on rules and organized control through the Catholic Church and more on their own personal relationships with God and the physical world. At the same time, as Europe became more accepting of other cultures and religions throughout the centuries, so too did the Knights Hospitaller.

Where does this leave the Order in the present day? Membership, while seemingly low, could be considered high given how many volunteers and medical staff continue to work with the Knights Hospitaller. Moreover, its mission is not as centralized but is far more encompassing and

---

[20] Guy Stair Sainty and Rafal Heydel-Mankoo eds., *World Orders of Knighthood and Merit*, (Wilmington: Burke's Peerage & Gentry, 2006).

beneficial to the world, focused less on bloodshed and more on assisting as many individuals as possible affected by warfare, natural disasters, and deadly diseases that can spread rapidly in less developed regions. As such, it can be argued that the Knights Hospitaller are now carrying on some of the best aspects of the original Crusades while leaving behind many of the negatives, resulting in the charitable and beneficial organization of the present day.

Online Resources

Other books about Catholic history by Charles River Editors

Other books about the Knights Hospitaller on Amazon

Bibliography

Allen, D.F. "Charles II, Louis XIV and the Order of Malta." *European History Quarterly*. 20 (3): April 2016, 323–340.

Arteaga, Deborah L. *Research on Old French: The State of the Art*. Springer Science & Business Media, 2012.

Balfour, Baron Kinross, Patrick. *The Ottoman Centuries: The Rise and Fall of the Turkish Empire*. Harper Collins, 1979.

Bamford, Paul Walden. "The Knights of Malta and the King of France, 1665-1700." *French Historical Studies*. 3 (4): Autumn 1964, 429–453.

Cole, Juan. *Napoleon's Egypt: Invading the Middle East*. Palgrave Macmillan, 2007.

Earle, Peter. *Corsairs of Malta and Barbary*. London: Sidgwick & Jackson, 1907.

Finkel, Caroline. *Osman's Dream: The Story of the Ottoman Empire, 1300-1923*. Basic Books, 2005.

Kollias, Elias. *The Knights of Rhodes – The Palace and the City*. 1991.

Lacroix, Paul. *Military and Religious Life in the Middle Ages and the Renaissance*. New York: Frederick Ungar, 1964.

Moeller, Charles. "Hospitallers of St. John of Jerusalem." In Herbermann, Charles. *Catholic Encyclopedia*. New York: Robert Appleton, 1913.

Nicholson, Helen J. *The Knights Hospitaller*. Woodbridge: The Boydell Press, 2001.

Rady, Martyn. *Nobility, Land and Service in Medieval Hungary*. Palgrave, 2000.

Riley-Smith, Jonathan. *Hospitallers: The History of the Order of St John*. Hambledon, 1999.

Riley-Smith, Jonathan Simon Christopher. *The Crusades, Christianity, and Islam*. Columbia University Press, 2013.

Robinson, J.H., ed. "The Decree Abolishing the Feudal System." *Readings in European History 2 vols*. Boston: Ginn. 2: 1906, 404–409.

Slack, Corliss K. *Historical Dictionary of the Crusades*. Scarecrow Press, 2013.

Sire, H. J. A. *The Knights of Malta*. Yale University Press, 1996.

Stair Sainty, Guy; Heydel-Mankoo, Rafal, eds. *World Orders of Knighthood and Merit*. Wilmington: Burke's Peerage & Gentry, 2006.

Sugden, John. *Nelson: The Sword of Albion*. Random House, 2014.

The Sovereign Military Hospitaller Order of St. John of Jerusalem of Rhodes and of Malta. *Special Review Commemorating the State Visit to Malta by His Most Eminent Highness The Prince and Grand Master Fra' Angelo de Mojana*. 1968.

Free Books by Charles River Editors

We have brand new titles available for free most days of the week. To see which of our titles are currently free, click on this link.

Discounted Books by Charles River Editors

We have titles at a discount price of just 99 cents everyday. To see which of our titles are currently 99 cents, click on this link.

Made in the USA
San Bernardino, CA
17 May 2020